To: Loretta and George,

Thank you so much for all the ways you have been friends to us over all these years. Enjoy this book from S. Rita. May her spirit live on as you read it.

Rita would want me to gift you with this in her memory and that of Thomasine and Johnelle.

My love,
S. Loretta

All Scriptural quotations are taken from
New Revised Standard Version Bible: Catholic Edition, copyright 1989, 1993.
Division of Christian Education of the National Council of the Churches of Christ
in the United States of America. Used by permission. All rights reserved.
Oxford University Press
Oxford – New York
Cardinal photo by Ralph W. Scott. Used with permission.

ISBN 0-9760534-8-9

Library of Congress Cataloging in Publication Data: 2004115686

  Barthel, Sister Rita, Finding Life's Purpose, Where Do I Encounter God?
  [1. Spirituality 2. Healing 3. Journaling 4. Religion 5. Conversion
  6. Meditation 7. Christianity]

Finding Life's Purpose

Where Do I Encounter God

Sister Rita Barthel, OSF

DEDICATION

To my friends who have taught me the wonders of life.

ACKNOWLEDGMENTS

Being privileged to walk side by side with people of all ages who have experienced the abundant joys as well as the intense sufferings of life, has inspired me to write about what gives purpose and meaning in life's journey.

To all who have enriched my life by sharing their journey, I am deeply grateful.

Perseverance in writing this book would not have happened without the encouragement of many friends and colleagues. I am particularly grateful to Pat Opatz, a writer, who in her dying months shared her insights and critique. My gratitude also goes to Mimi Bitzan, Terry Sakry, Tom and Dorothy Noud and Margaret Heydman, who painstakingly read and re-read the script and offered wonderful ideas and suggestions. I would also like to acknowledge others who shared their helpful comments and insights: Delores Hiemenz, Ron Schmelzer, Jim Neppl, Sister Elise Saggau, Lynne Lindmeier and many members of my Franciscan Community.

CONTENTS

Introduction

Part One: The Brightness of Our Earthly Paradise   pg 1

Becoming more aware of God's presence in the beauty of creation and in the people around us helps us celebrate the simple and exquisite gifts of everyday life and reminds us of God's ever-present love — even when times are difficult.

Part Two: The Darkness of Our Earthly Paradise   pg 22

Reflecting on the steps of the journey Jesus took on his way towards Calvary reminds us that as followers of Christ, we are called to walk these same steps. What is the meaning of "The Way of the Cross" for each of us?

Part Three: The Heavenly Paradise, Our Destiny   pg 43

Do I wait in joyful hope and in anticipation of my final destiny — heaven? Embrace God's promises of love and reflect with faith on what heaven may be like.

Part Four: Witnesses of Faith, Hope and Love   pg 50

Stories of extra-ordinary wisdom from ordinary people offer insight and inspiration as we continue on our own journey of faith.

INTRODUCTION

"In our eagerness to learn things quickly
we take crash courses,
but the truly important things in life are
learned slowly,
with a great deal of reflection and prayer."

~ Sister Rita Barthel, OSF ~

In our search for happiness, fulfillment and the desire to accomplish great things in life, we are easily lured by outward glamour, pleasure, success, accomplishments, the exhilarating experience of being in control and possessing a super abundance of material things. These drives relate to the basic desires of the human heart that seek to be satisfied. Some of these desires include the desire for happiness, the desire to love and be loved, the desire for safety and security, the desire to be successful, and the desire to be free and live fully and forever. When we strive to satisfy these desires only on a human level we come to a point where the satisfaction ends, especially when we are faced with poor health, crises of any kind, old age and death. It is often during these difficult times that we are awakened to a deeper spiritual reality that opens our minds and hearts to reflect more intently on the purpose of our life here on this earth.

FINDING LIFE'S PURPOSE, WHERE DO I ENCOUNTER GOD? is designed to help us see and appreciate, at every moment of our life, the goodness and beauty of life, the reality of suffering and its meaning, and the hope to which we are called.

This book is not for speed-readers. It is not a cookbook or "how to" book. Rather, it is a book whose pages are to be pondered, not just once, but over and over again. We learn slowly how to walk through life with mindfulness and how to cooperate with our God. It takes time, reflection and repeated effort to find the deeper meaning, purpose and beauty of the mystery of life and to understand what these mean for us on our own unique and very special journey. It is my hope that these reflections will help the reader discover how all of life's experiences lead us to where we are at this moment, to search more deeply, and to understand more fully, the purpose of our own earthly journey.

The pages of this book present the multitudinous gifts and wonders in the world around us that we, perhaps, take for granted or have not paused to enjoy. The reflections on these pages call us to see and hear with inner eyes and ears to capture the depth of beauty and the significance of these marvels as well as to realize the oneness of all of life. They help us recognize that struggles, limitations and suffering are part of the human condition — and that, as people of faith, we courageously walk this human journey with hope, knowing that ultimately all will be well as we rise to new life. These pages call us to wait in joyful hope and anticipation of our final destiny and present true stories of faith, hope and love that make us realize we are extraordinarily ordinary people who are truly unique and precious because we are made in the image and likeness of God. One can reflect on any page at any given moment, to find strength in a special need.

As you immerse in the pages that follow, consider taking time for personal journaling, sharing your reflections with a prayer partner or small group, or going apart to make a quiet retreat.

The stories and faith journeys of holy people can inspire us on our own journey of faith.

Sister Rita Barthel, OSF

The Brightness of Our Earthly Paradise

Often the question is asked: "Where is God when I am in need?" This query reveals an all too common reality, and I find it also surfacing in my own life. Do I expect my God to simply be a provider for my needs in times of crisis? I do believe that God desires a deep love relationship with each person on earth, and like in any other relationship, it takes time to come to know the intimate ways in which that relationship is revealed and expressed. With the eyes of the heart we can find God's expression of love in the beauty of the earth and human interaction.

Walk With Joy

I walk with joy in this paradise on earth, and I know in faith that my God walks with me. I am one with the universe, and all creation contributes to the unfolding of my life. The experience of the splendor of beauty, the magnificence of action and interaction, the quiet, hidden growth within me quicken my soul.

I will place my dwelling in your midst, and I shall not abhor you. And I will walk among you, and will be your God, and you shall be my people. Lv. 26:11-12

Reflection:

When or where do I feel God's presence most strongly?

What is my relationship with creation?
What is my relationship with others?
What is my relationship with God?

What experiences in my life bring me joy?

Experience:

Sit in a quiet place and imagine that Jesus is sitting next to you.
Talk to him about your joys in life. Then sit in stillness and simply be present.

Gifts of Love

When living in harmony with others and with creation, I find God's gifts of love hidden in the simple and ordinary happenings of life. These gifts are manifested in the smile of a stranger, an unexpected thank you, the gift of a loaf of fresh bread or home-baked cookies, the blossoming of a flower, the growth in a garden and the sharing with friends. Slowly I learn to recognize the extra-ordinary in the ordinary happenings of life. In the stories of God's love, as told by the lowly, humble and suffering, I hear God's voice.

How precious is your steadfast love, O God! All people may take refuge in the shadow of your wings.
They feast on the abundance of your house, and you give them drink from the river of your delights. Ps. 36:7-8

Reflection:

In what ways do I experience God's love?

What gifts has God given me? In what ways do I show my gratitude for God's gifts?

Experience:

Write down ten things you are grateful for since you got out of bed this morning.

Review the list before going to bed and give thanks to God. Continue this practice for one week. In what ways have your appreciation and awareness of God's gifts changed?

Songs of Love

Through the plaintive voice of the loon, the whistle of the cardinal, the tweet of the wren, and the raucous melody of the blackbird, God sings songs of love to me to awaken my soul.

My beloved speaks and says to me: 'Arise, my love, my fair one, and come away; Song of Solomon 2:10

Reflection:

What awakens my soul to God?

When have I heard God singing to me?

How do I begin my day?

Experience:

As you get up in the morning, sit on the bed and listen for the sounds in nature. Turn to the east, bow to the dawn and ask to hear God's songs of love through the day.

Rays of the Sun

By the rays of the sun, God gives warmth, light and energy to my body and lifts my spirit to be fully alive and marked with glory. I, in turn, can shine like the sun to reveal God's radiance and light. God's beauty and presence are experienced in light: in the vivid colors of a sunrise or sunset, in the glistening leaves after a rainfall, in the stars at night, in the way a child's eyes light up.

For with you is the fountain of life; in your light we see light. Ps. 36:9

Reflection:

In what ways do I receive God's light, warmth and energy?

How am I being called to reflect God's light, warmth and energy to others?

Experience:

When talking with someone today, be especially conscious of being present to them and looking into their eyes. What is the light you see there?

God's Energy and Delight

The ripples of the lake's water remind me that life is swirling with energy and delight. Throughout my life, God dances around me in rhythmic flow and constant movement, filling me with energy.

More majestic than the thunders of mighty waters, more majestic than the waves of the sea, majestic on high is the Lord. Ps. 93:4

Reflection:

God fills me with energy. I think of the times when I have felt God's energy:
in times of inspiration, insight and beauty,
in times of sadness, pain, patience grown thin,
in times of prayer.

In what other specific events or circumstances have I felt God's energy?

Experience:

Reach out with kindness today to someone who is tired, sad or lonely.
Share the energy of your love and care.

Born of the Spirit

The breezes touch and refresh my body and spirit. Like the air that cannot be seen, yet felt, so it is with the presence of God's Spirit.

The wind blows where it chooses, and you hear the sound of it, but you do not know where it comes from or where it goes. So it is with everyone who is born of the Spirit. Jn. 3:8

Reflection:

What would I do without air? Without God?

How do I respect air and keep it clean for all peoples and creatures?

When have I been guided by the Spirit or responded to the prompting of the Spirit: in a decision I have made, in a phone call placed, in an invitation of a neighbor to dinner, in a visit to the sick or lonely, in helping a stranger?

Experience:

Do something new and different today that will refresh someone's spirits.

Beauty of God

In the bright-eyed daisy, the cascading bleeding heart, the delicate bridal wreath and the stately iris, the beauty of God bursts open for me to fill my soul with wonder and awe.

One thing I asked of the Lord, that will I seek after; to live in the house of the Lord all the days of my life, to behold the beauty of the Lord, and to inquire in his temple. Ps. 27:4

Reflection:

What beauty have I delighted in today?

In what ways has God's love blossomed within me?

What is beautiful about me?

What is beautiful about the people I love? Name their gifts.

Experience:

Affirm others today for their beauty, gifts, or for something they have accomplished.

God's Mighty Trees

God's mighty trees of whistling pine, peaceful oak, swaying weeping willow and trembling aspen offer brave strongholds that give me inspiration, shelter and strength.

Blessed are those who trust in the Lord, whose trust is the Lord. They shall be like a tree planted by water, sending out its roots by the stream. It shall not fear when heat comes, and its leaves shall stay green; in the year of drought it is not anxious, and it does not cease to bear fruit. Jer. 17:7-8

Reflection:

In what ways am I like a tree?

Do I have roots that anchor me firmly?

Do I have branches that reach out to others?

Am I like a willow that easily bends and is not rigid?

Am I like a pine tree that is always green and fresh?

Am I like a mighty oak that is strong in the face of any trial?

Experience:

Take time to contemplate a tree. Sit in front of the tree.
Study the branches and leaves.
Observe the movement of the tree.
Touch the trunk of the tree.
What does this tree teach you about God?

Nourishment

Myriads of foods: Crunchy orange carrots, lily white potatoes, mild green onions, juicy red strawberries, and sweet pastel melons are gifts from God that delight my palate and fill and nourish me.

You cause the grass to grow for the cattle, and plants for people to use, to bring forth food from the earth, and wine to gladden the human heart, oil to make the face shine, and bread to strengthen the human heart. Ps. 104:14-15

Reflection:

How do I show my appreciation for God's great variety of foods and drink?

In what ways do I share and nourish those around me:
by my support, by my caring,
by my feeding the hungry,
by my prayer?

Experience:

Write a blessing and pray it before eating a meal.
Eat the meal slowly and savor the taste and texture of the food.
Pray a prayer of thanksgiving after the meal.

Generous Listener

The God-given capacity to be a generous listener, a caring friend and a comforting presence, helps me to share myself and God's gift of love with others. Others, in return, share themselves and God's gifts with me.

Cure the sick, raise the dead, cleanse the lepers, cast out demons. You received without payment; give without payment. Mt. 10:8

Reflection:

Who is in need of my listening presence and support?

What is my ability to love in the grip of anger, fear, abuse or violence?

Who has gifted me with his/her presence and been a generous listener?

Experience:

Send your healing power of understanding and care to someone you know who feels misunderstood and rejected.

Tender Touch

The arms of those who love me—
the warm embrace of parents and grandparents,
the jovial hugs of brothers and sisters,
the faithful embrace of friends,
the joining of hands in prayer—
are ways God embraces and holds me.
As I experience the touch and tenderness of the care of others, my love deepens.

Owe no one anything, except to love one another; for the one who loves another has fulfilled the law. Rom. 13:8

Reflection:

In what ways do I express my love for God?

How do I express my love for others?

Experience:

Visit someone who is ill and pray together if desired.
Offer to hold hands as you pray.

Be Still

Long nights of dream-filled sleep, short daytime naps, deep pauses of stillness, provide restoration to my body so I can live each new day with renewed vigor.

Be still, and know that I am God! I am exalted among the nations; I am exalted in the earth. Ps. 46:10

Reflection:

Where are you able to rest in the presence of God?

In what ways does rest refresh you?

Experience:

Go to a favorite place such as a church, lake or special room.
For twenty minutes be still and listen to God's voice within you.
How does this experience affect your day?

The Wonders of Music

The wonders of music lift my spirit and gladden my heart: the music of the human voice, the music of a choral group, the music of violin, harp, organ, flute, piano, dulcimer, saxophone, trumpet and many more. The wonders of music touch the strings of my heart to make music within me. Music lifts my spirit to my Creator in praise and thanksgiving for God's steadfast love.

Sing aloud to God our strength; shout for joy to the God of Jacob. Raise a song, sound the tambourine, the sweet lyre with the harp. Blow the trumpet at the new moon, at the full moon, on our festal day. Ps. 81:1-3

Reflection:

When was a time that music comforted my spirits?

What part does music play in my daily life?

Experience:

Relax and play some soft, inspirational music. As you listen, let go of any feelings of disharmony or anxiety. Let the beauty of the music cleanse your spirit of all that is negative or worrisome and allow it to bring light, restfulness and love.

Bread of Life

In the celebration of Eucharist, I experience the presence of Christ in the reality of the here and now. Through the Word of God from Sacred Scripture, God's presence shapes and transforms my inner life and reminds me that I am made in the image of God.

When participating in Eucharist, I know of Christ's sacrifice and love. I receive Christ, the Bread of Life, who nourishes me, increases Christ's life within me and gives me courage, energy, enthusiasm and compassion for my daily journey.

Eucharist connects me to people everywhere – to the world's poor and hungry, to the sick and dying, to the lonely and bereaved — and sends me forth to be Christ to them.

For I received from the Lord what I also handed on to you, that the Lord Jesus on the night when he was betrayed took a loaf of bread, and when he had given thanks, he broke it and said, 'This is my body that is for you. Do this in remembrance of me.' In the same way he took the cup also, after supper, saying, 'This cup is the new covenant in my blood. Do this, as often as you drink it, in remembrance of me.' For as often as you eat this bread and drink the cup, you proclaim the Lord's death until he comes. 1 Cor. 11:23-25

Reflection:

Jesus said to them, 'I am the bread of life. Whoever comes to me will never be hungry, and whoever believes in me will never be thirsty.' Jn. 6:35

Do you believe that Jesus is the true bread from heaven?

How does Jesus feed you?

In what way can I be the presence of Christ for someone today?

Where have I encountered Christ today?

Experience:

Imagine being at the Last Supper with Jesus, hearing his words:
"Take and eat, this is my body." Think of these words as an invitation to be one with Jesus. See yourself as being transformed and becoming like Jesus in his great love, self-giving and compassion.

Plan a specific action:
Do something to increase your awareness of Christ's presence.
Treat those around you as if they were Christ.
Reach out to someone you don't know well.
Greet a stranger as a brother or sister.

Sacraments of Life and Strength

Other sacraments of Christ's love are gifts that offer me new life and strength: the waters of Christ's life, reconciliation to mend my brokenness and wounded relationships, the oil of healing, constant enlightenment and the power of the Spirit through the gifts of Wisdom, Understanding, Right Judgment, Courage, Knowledge, Reverence, Wonder and Awe.

Every generous act of giving, with every perfect gift, is from above, coming down from the Father of lights, with whom there is no variation or shadow due to change. Jas. 1:17

Reflection:

A sacrament is an outward sign of an inward grace or blessing.
What are the "sacraments" in my life?

When was a time that the celebration of a sacrament held special meaning for me? Why?

What changes have occurred in my life because of the celebration of a sacrament?

Experience:

Avail yourself of the Rite of Reconciliation and look upon it as an encounter with God. Attend a Baptism and give thanks for your own Baptism and life in God. Speak to a Confirmation Candidate and express your own appreciation of the gifts of the Holy Spirit.

Ask, and You Shall Receive

I remember that God has walked this way before me and I need not fear. I have hope that God will satisfy my every desire.

Deep peace of the running wave to you... Deep peace of the flowing air to you...
Deep peace of the quiet earth to you... Deep peace of the shining stars to you...
Deep peace of the gentle night to you... Moon and stars pour their healing light on you...
Deep peace to you...
Anonymous Celtic Blessing

'Ask, and it will be given to you; search, and you will find; knock, and the door will be opened for you. For everyone who asks receives, and everyone who searches finds, and for everyone who knocks, the door will be opened'. Mt. 7:7-8

Reflection:

What do I believe God promises me?

What desires do I have at this time that I would like satisfied?

What are my deepest hopes?

Experience:

Meditate on Jesus' words: "Ask and you shall receive."
Ask God to give you your heart's greatest desire.

An Invitation to Journal...

An Invitation to Journal...

The Darkness of Our Earthly Paradise

In this earthly paradise the brightness and abundance of God's gifts are, at times, clouded with darkness. I find that I must walk the way of the cross of suffering, weakness and doubt.

In the Roman Catholic tradition, Jesus' way of the cross is marked by fourteen stations, the significant steps of Jesus' journey toward Calvary. As a follower of Christ I am called to walk in His footsteps.

First Station

Jesus is Condemned to Death

I must die one day because it is the way of all human life.

I realize that I must accept the journey of my way of the cross.

Often throughout my life I die a little when I must let go of things I treasure.

I must let go of doing things my way.

I must let go of good health when I get sick.

I must let go of my children when they become adults.

I must let go of neighbors when they move away.

I must let go of my job when I am laid off.

I must let go of loved ones when they die.

I remember that I am a spiritual being living in a physical body. Suffering is only a small part of my earthly life. It reminds me to turn to my spiritual life for comfort and healing.

Even though I walk through the darkest valley, I fear no evil; for you are with me; your rod and your staff—they comfort me. Ps. 23:4

Reflection:

When have I experienced a loss or a letting go?

What is my attitude toward human suffering and pain?

What value, if any, do I see in suffering?

What can suffering teach me?

What fears do I have about death?

How can I prepare myself now for my final "letting go"?

Experience:

Visit someone who has experienced loss or is suffering.
Be willing to share this persons pain, sitting together in the darkness.

Second Station

Jesus Carries His Cross

The cross of being human is placed upon my shoulders as I journey to my heavenly paradise. It is the cross of incompleteness, weakness. I carry the cross of human limitation, financial stress, health problems, worries, fears and doubts.

And we urge you, beloved, to admonish the idlers, encourage the fainthearted, help the weak, be patient with all of them. 1 Thes. 5:14

Reflection:

What are my human limitations?

What do I find difficult to accept about myself?

If I could change something about myself, what would it be?

What limitations in others do I find difficult to accept?

What is my attitude toward having to carry a cross?

Experience:

Name your greatest limitations or a cross you are carrying now.

Sit in prayer and ask God to be present with you today as you carry this cross.

Third Station
Jesus Falls the First Time Under His Cross

I stumble and fall because of my imperfections, but I have hope in the goodness of being human. I trust that the strength of God within me will help me to get up and carry on.

The sacrifice acceptable to God is a broken spirit; a broken and contrite heart, O God, you will not despise. Ps. 51:17

Reflection:

In what ways am I stumbling now in my life?

What is causing me to fall or fail?

Admitting my faults or shortcomings is difficult for me to do.
When I do, I often grow.
When do I find it most difficult to acknowledge my mistakes
and imperfections? Why?

Experience:

Think about one area of your life you want to improve.
Share your desires with a trusted friend or spiritual director.

Fourth Station

Jesus Meets His Afflicted Mother

I meet my mother, the embodiment of love.
Her eyes meet mine, and somehow I know that all will be well.

And why has this happened to me, that the mother of my Lord comes to me? Lk. 1:43

Reflection:

Who is it that mothers me in times of stress and anguish?

Mary does not turn away from Jesus' suffering. She faces her pain and his.
How am I able to comfort others on their journey of suffering?

Experience:

Remember the love your mother showed you in some incidents in your life. Absorb
the warmth and energy you recall. What was her love like? Ask her to help you
be faithful, strong and daring in living and acting as Jesus would live and act. Ask
her to give you courage in suffering. If she is still living, tell her "Thank you".

The Fifth Station

Simon of Cyrene Helps Jesus Carry His Cross

There are friends and companions on my journey:

those who cry with me when I am sad,

those who stand by me in troubled times,

those who laugh with me when joy fills my life,

those who help me carry my cross when the burdens of life weigh me down,

and those who act as advocates in my stead.

When suffering is shared it is lessened.

When joy is shared it is increased.

If one member suffers, all suffer together with it; if one member is honored, all rejoice together with it. 1 Cor. 12:26

Reflection:

Whose burdens am I being asked to lighten right now?

Experience:

Be attentive and anticipate the needs of those who live in your household:
a spouse, a child, a brother or sister. Observe any stress, worry, fear or difficulty in
accomplishing a task that they may have. Help them in a way you see fit. Carry
this attentiveness to your place of work.

Sixth Station

Veronica Wipes the Face of Jesus

When sweating and in pain a loved one wipes my face.
I give in return an imprint of my soul, telling of my destiny as a child of God.

This is my comfort in my distress, that your promise gives me life. Ps. 119:50

Reflection:

How do I feel when my offers of caring and comfort are accepted by another?

In what ways have I felt the comfort and care of others?

What promises of God give me hope in the midst of suffering
and difficult times?

Experience:

Visit someone you know who has a terminal illness. Ask the person if there is a way
in which you can be of help. Invite the person to share fears or difficulties. Promise
your prayer, love and support. Ask if you can pray and let your prayer reflect what
has been shared.

Seventh Station

Jesus Falls a Second Time

In my weakness I fall again.
My selfishness, impatience and misunderstanding drag
me down in my relationships with others.
With courage I must admit and accept the human limitations and
sinfulness that cause me to fall again.

As God's chosen ones, holy and beloved, clothe yourselves with compassion, kindness, humility, meekness, and patience. Bear with one another and, if anyone has a complaint against another, forgive each other; just as the Lord has forgiven you, so you also must forgive. Above all, clothe yourselves with love, which binds everything together in perfect harmony. Col. 3:12-14

Reflection:

For what and from whom do I need to ask forgiveness?

Whom do I need to forgive?

Experience:

Make a conscious effort to be aware of when your actions or words hurt others.
Acknowledge it.

Eighth Station

Jesus Meets the Weeping Women of Jerusalem

I meet people in my world who weep because of their sins or their inadequacies and the evil that exists in the world.

Weeping for ourselves and others is necessary in our world of weakness, injustice and hatred.

Yet even now, says the Lord, return to me with all your heart, with fasting, with weeping, and with mourning.
Joel 2:12

Reflection:

What situations in my life or in the world are calling me to weep?

Experience:

Write down two situations that cause you to weep. Pray about them for one week. Read the Gospel for each day of the week and reflect on how it speaks to the situations you've written about.

Ninth Station

Jesus Falls a Third Time

Exhausted and overcome with trial,
I fall again.
Life has become wild with frenzied, urgent rushing feet. There is no solitude.
I call upon God to set me on the right path once again.

Do not adorn yourselves outwardly by braiding your hair, and by wearing gold ornaments or fine clothing; rather, let your adornment be the inner self with the lasting beauty of a gentle and quiet spirit, which is very precious in God's sight. 1 Peter 3:3-4

Reflection:

How do I center myself and regain my balance when my world appears to be falling apart?

Experience:

Meditate for five minutes on the phrase: "God provides for me."

Tenth Station

Jesus is Stripped of His Garments

Life strips me of my garments: my pride, my friends,
my bodily youthfulness, my dignity, my health, my being in control,
my independence, my having things perfect,
my being included, my ability to think and remember,
my eyesight, and my desire to live my life to the fullest and enjoy every moment.
My God, I stand naked before you, but it is all right because I remember that I am
your beloved.

Then Job arose, tore his robe, shaved his head, and fell on the ground and worshipped. He said, 'Naked I came from my mother's womb, and naked shall I return there; the Lord gave, and the Lord has taken away; blessed be the name of the Lord'. Job 1:20-21

Reflection:

What is my attitude toward human life as I deal with sickness, misfortune or old age?

How do my losses teach me to trust?

Who in my life is struggling with loss?

Reflection:

What can I do to offer them hope and to show them they are God's beloved?

What greater treasures might one gain when stripped of earthly treasures?

Experience:

Write a litany of your "losses" and respond after each loss listed:
"God, help me to trust in you."
Examples:
I lost my job.
I am no longer able to sleep well at night.
My grandmother and friend has died.

Eleventh Station

Jesus is Nailed to the Cross

I am nailed to a cross. I cannot move and I am in utter anguish. God are you with me in this darkness? My sin and failure cause me excruciating suffering. My physical sickness and pain cause me anguish. In time of desperate need, I turn to you. Let me see your goodness and glory. I stake my claim on your Word. God, let me be led by love and not by fear, so I may experience the power of your care.

I consider that the sufferings of this present time are not worth comparing with the glory about to be revealed to us. Rom. 8:18

Reflection:

In what ways does suffering force me to think beyond my bodily pain?

What have I done to help myself through times of great suffering?

What have others done to help me through times of suffering?

Experience:

Sit in a quiet place. Close your eyes. Be aware of your breathing as the very breath of God. As you inhale, breathe in God's love. As you exhale, breathe out the pain or suffering. Feel yourself surrounded by God's all-embracing love.

Twelfth Station

Jesus Dies on the Cross

My God, have you abandoned me?

Will I die on this cross?

What will happen when I die?

I remember that death is but a movement from one type of existence to another.

God, can I persevere in my faith, hope and love for you?

Suffering and death remind me of my dependence on you, O God.

Help me to believe that you are present with me in my pain and help me to see the truth of your love for me.

May I never boast of anything except the cross of our Lord Jesus Christ, by which the world has been crucified to me, and I to the world. Gal. 6:14

Reflection:

Have I ever felt abandoned by God? When?

How does faith, acceptance and even humor help me deal with suffering in ways that are healthy rather than destructive?

How can suffering open my heart to God's love?

Experience:

Sometimes in the face of loss or death, it is helpful to repeat a short prayer to comfort one's spirit. Hold a crucifix in your hand, gaze on it and spend five to ten minutes saying one of the following prayers over and over.

+ O my God, help me in this moment of anguish.

+ O God, you are my life and my hope.

+ Lord Jesus, have mercy on me.

Thirteenth Station

Jesus is Taken Down From the Cross and Placed in the Arms of His Mother

My life is changed and my suffering is ended.

I surrender my life to you, O God. I rest in you.

Friends come and lovingly hold my body.

They experience with me the relief from my suffering, yet grieve at parting.

Those I leave behind will carry on and will know that love never dies.

And I heard a voice from heaven saying, 'Write this: Blessed are the dead who from now on die in the Lord.' 'Yes,' says the Spirit, 'they will rest from their labours, for their deeds follow them.' Rev. 14:13

Reflection:

What are the greatest lessons I have learned on this earthly journey?

How have I shared these learnings with others?

Experience:

Spend some time reflecting and writing down the greatest lessons you have learned in life and plan to share them with family members.

Fourteenth Station

Jesus is Placed in the Tomb

Like Jesus, my body will be laid to rest. Resting from all suffering and struggle is not yet the end. This pain and even seeming despair are only shadows of darkness in this earthly paradise and they will pass away.

Truly the eye of the Lord is on those who fear him, on those who hope in his steadfast love, to deliver their soul from death, and to keep them alive in famine. Ps. 33:18-19

Reflection:

When I am gone, what do I hope others will remember about me?

What messages do I wish to leave behind?

What am I doing now to insure that a clear message will be left behind?

What are my prayers for those I will leave behind?

Experience:

Write out a wish or a prayer for each of your loved ones.

An Invitation to Journal...

An Invitation to Journal...

The Heavenly Paradise, Our Destiny

Do I wait in joyful hope and in anticipation of my final destiny – heaven? This might be easier to do if I did not have to pass through the unknown portals of death. Yet, how am I to prepare myself for this passing, which is the greatest and most important moment of my life?

This reality is faced by people of all ages – a teenager who undergoes a serious car accident, a middle-aged person who has a rare disease, a person who has just retired and realized that the greater part of life has been lived, or an older person who knows that the number of years on earth is limited. But should we not all be asking this question, regardless of our age or circumstance in life? Surely to die well depends on whether I have lived well. What does living well mean?

If I search the Scriptures I will find some clear essentials to living a good and holy life.

Faith is a basic and primary requisite – faith in a God who loves, heals, watches over, guides, and empowers me. Hope is also necessary – a hope in God's promises for a life of eternal happiness which begins already here on earth. The most essential is love – a love which encompasses an intimate relationship with God, as well as a love for every other person as brother and sister.

God has gifted me with these basic gifts but it is my responsibility to open my heart so that the Spirit of God can bring them to fruition. I need to ask the Holy Spirit daily to make my faith more firm, to make my hope more confident and to make my love more ardent.

The Glory of God Awaits

The God of Glory awaits my coming home to the heavenly paradise where I will rise again to live in love with God forever.

God's infinite love is the greatest treasure I possess, and this love, holiness and goodness will be shared by everyone in our heavenly paradise.

My eyes have not seen, nor have my ears heard about the wonders that God has ready for me.

'Who is like you, O Lord, among the gods? Who is like you, majestic in holiness, awesome in splendour, doing wonders?' Ex. 15:11

Reflection:

St. Augustine says: "You have made us for yourself, O God, and our hearts are restless until they rest in you." What in my life leaves me feeling restless?

Is the thought of death frightening or consoling for me? Why?

Do I talk about death with those I love?

Experience:

Heaven is a place of love and heaven begins here on earth. For one day, practice seeing the good in everyone and in everything, and do not allow yourself to focus on anything negative or bad. Awaken your heart to see God's love everywhere, even in sickness and suffering.

Picture of Heaven

What are the wonders God has ready for me?
Would it not be true that:

- if I am in the presence of the ones I dearly love on earth, I will live in joy and bliss with them in heaven?

- if I have loved others – a spouse, children, brothers, sisters, relatives, friends, the poor and needy— the God of love will reunite me with them?

- if I have delighted in beauty, truth and goodness, I will glory in these realities even more in eternity?

- if I have loved the adventure of learning, I will continue to delight in learning?

- if I have cherished the mysteries of life, I will stand in awe of their secrets? If I have loved to sing and dance, I will continue to sing and dance for joy for all eternity with all my loved ones, the saints and angels?

- if I have shared my treasures, talents and time, I will share in the abundance of the treasures and creativity of others for all eternity?

My soul thirsts for God, for the living God. When shall I come and behold the face of God? Ps. 42:2

Reflection:

As I think about my life, the people in it, my own special talents, gifts and the events which have brought me to this day, what do I perceive to be my life's purpose?

In what ways have I fulfilled this purpose and what have I yet to do?

What do I believe in or hope for on this next phase of my journey?

What questions do I have for God?

Experience:

Write about your picture of heaven. Include what you believe to be the most essential realities of heaven.

An Invitation to Journal...

An Invitation to Journal...

Witness of Faith, Hope and Love

I wait in joyful anticipation to enter into the fullness of life and love.

In my ministry I've discovered that common people have uncommon wisdom and profound insight and faith. People give marvelous witness to their faith, hope and love as they delight in the goodness of life, endure suffering and anticipate the glory to come. It is evident that many virtues are an integral part of their way of life and it is a profound inspiration to witness their goodness and holiness of life.

In the following true stories we uncover some of the wisdom of everyday people with everyday strength and joys — some of whom have now died, some who are very alive and active and some who are nearing the end of their earthly journey and preparing to arrive at their final destiny.

Have a Good Day

Al was having a bad day, or so it seemed to me from outward appearances. He was sick in the hospital with a heart problem. Yet Al was telling me about the good nurses who were caring for him and he could not say enough about their kindness and pleasant demeanor. Al thought that even the food was good in this hospital. "I have a beautiful view from my window," he exclaimed, "and this morning I was watching the cloud formations through my window. I love to hear the sound of the birds. My wife was here to see me earlier. Oh, she is a wonderful woman. All my children have been up to see me, too. I'm so proud of them."

I prayed with Al and when I was ready to leave he said: "Have a good day, and if it is not good, enjoy it anyway."

Wisdom shared: "If it is not good, enjoy it anyway."

Al had learned in his life to look for goodness.
Instead of concentrating on the negative, he found love everywhere.

I'll Be Sending You Messages

My sister, Bernadette, sent me a birthday card from Texas the day before she died. I received it in Minnesota three days later and at the end of her birthday greetings she wrote: "I'll be sending you messages." Why did she say that?

That afternoon as I was feeding the birds, a cardinal came and perched on a limb of the pine tree and began singing. It sang on and on for about ten minutes. I walked toward it and it continued to sit there and sing. Suddenly it dawned on me that this was Bernadette's first message to me. " I am happy, I am singing and life is beautiful." I believe our loved ones who have died have moved into a fuller life and are closer to us than we can ever imagine. Have you felt the presence of a loved one who has died?

Wisdom Shared: "I'll be sending you messages."

There is another dimension of being that is beyond our human existence and yet still closely connected with life here on earth. This spiritual realm is the fullness of God's life, love, beauty and joy which we share.

Do Not Let Me Forget That God Loves Me

Walter's wife had died some years ago and now Walter was home struggling with cancer. Each time I visited him he seemed weaker and I knew it was time for a heart to heart talk. In Walter's lifetime he had spent many hours befriending people who were sick or lonely, so it was only right that he now receive the comfort he needed.

Instead of presuming I knew what he most needed I decided to ask: "Walter, tell me, what is the most important thing I can do for you at this time?" His answer was immediate: "Pray with me often. I need so much encouragement each day, each hour. Talk to me and let me tell you about what is happening to me day by day. Let me tell you about my fears, about my pain and suffering. Let me complain a little but encourage me to hang on to the hand of Jesus. Remind me to offer up my suffering because it has value and purpose. It is sometimes difficult to remember this in the midst of pain. I know that God loves me, but I seem to forget that so quickly."

Wisdom Shared: "I need so much encouragement each day, each hour."

Walter reminded me to give my friendship, listening ear, spiritual support, hope and prayer to those who are in need. This is true companionship of souls.

A Gift

My sister, Bernadine, was fifty-three years old when she was told she had five tumors on her liver. The prognosis was not good. Family, relatives and numerous friends began to pray fervently for her to be healed. The tumors began to shrink and she was feeling well and full of energy. This lasted for three years, and during this time many people with cancer came to her for comfort and support. Then the cancer returned and spread to the bones. Her bones began to break and Bernadine was in great pain.

When talking with her one day I asked: "What is it like to live with cancer and to suffer all this pain?" After a long pause she said: "You know, my cancer has been a gift to me." "Gift?" I asked. I was not ready to hear this, nor was I willing to accept it. "Oh," she said, "you must understand that the pain of being ill, the lack of energy to be with my husband and family and having to let go of the hope of seeing my grandchildren grow up are terrible losses for me. The gift of my illness, however, is that I have come to know God in a way I have never known God before. Psalm 23 may help you understand what I mean. It is my constant prayer.

"The Lord is my shepherd, I shall not want. He makes me lie down in green pastures; he leads me beside still waters; he restores my soul. He leads me in right paths for his name's sake. Even though I walk through the darkest valley, I fear no evil; for you are with me; your rod and your staff—they comfort me.

You prepare a table before me in the presence of my enemies; you anoint my head with oil; my cup overflows. Surely goodness and mercy shall follow me all the days of my life, and I shall dwell in the house of the Lord my whole life long."

As we shared how we understood each aspect of this prayer, I came to realize how her "cup overflows" with a new life filled with God's love.

A large banner, made for her funeral, still hangs on a wall in her home with this passage from Scripture: "I walk in the presence of the Lord in the land of the living." Ps. 116:9.

Wisdom Shared: "The gift of my illness is that I have come to know God in a way I have never known God before."

God's love was Bernadine's strength and joy and her cancer helped her to depend on that love in a profound and new way.

My Happiest Day of Life

"The day of my death will be the happiest day of my life," says Anna. Anna is bedridden and has been at death's door several times. She says: "It is when I am facing death that I truly understand why Jesus suffered and showed me how to die. I don't have to die alone because Jesus is right there with me."

One day when visiting with Anna, she seemed sad. I asked her if something was bothering her. "Yes," she said, "I've been thinking about my relationship with Jesus. I can say that I love Jesus, but I don't think I have 'fallen in love' with Jesus. I guess I'm not ready to die because I don't love God enough yet."

When Anna talks about her funeral she says she wants the funeral liturgy to be a joyous celebration. She chose a hymn that called for people to dance in the presence of God. "Dance, then, wherever you may be. I am the Lord of the dance, said he. I'll lead you all, wherever you may be. I'll lead you all in the dance, said he."

Anna allows God to lead her in the dance of life, even through many years of suffering. Anna likes to share the quote from St. Augustine with her friends:

"Learn to dance, otherwise the angels in heaven won't know what to do with you."

Anna says to her family and friends: "It will not be too difficult for me to say good-bye when the day of death comes, because I'll see you all again soon."

Wisdom Shared: "Learn to dance."

Anna shows us how to live with a deep sense of joy. Even in her sickness, life is a dance and a celebration for her because she knows God is with her and loves her.

Peace in the Midst of Pain

Annie was lying on the davenport in her home. She was tired and in pain. She shared the struggle of having no cure in sight and of her sense of discouragement in the dark days. A look of panic came over her as she expressed her fear: "I'm so afraid I will die alone." Annie had been an orphan.

We prayed together and when we were finished she said: "These blessings wear off quickly, come again soon." Then in a quiet but strong voice she added: "I must also tell you that even in the midst of my pain and panic, I feel a deep peace and comfort in my heart. I know it is a power from outside of me. I know it is Jesus who embraces me with love."

Wisdom Shared: "I know it is Jesus who embraces me with love."

Jesus reveals himself and gives the graces we need in times of struggle. Annie was given peace and comfort.

Is It Worth It?

Rhea was a woman in her nineties. Up until two weeks before her death she was reading the WALL STREET JOURNAL and keeping up with world events and baseball. She was a woman who spoke her mind and it was always a delight to converse with her.

When I arrived at the nursing home one day and asked about Rhea, I was told that she was in a coma. I went to stand by her bed and called her name, "Rhea." Slowly she opened her eyes and looked at me. "Sister, is it worth it?" She asked. I was confused. "What do you mean, 'is it worth it'?" "Oh," she said: "I know I'm dying and I'm afraid. I doubt everything I ever believed. I wonder if this is just plain 'the end.'" "How could it just all end, Rhea!" I replied. "All your life you believed in God. Do you believe God loves you?" I asked. "Well, yes," she said, " I think God loves me and I have tried to love God, my husband and other people. Will God forgive all my sins?" She asked. She then continued: "As I lie here, all I can think of is how bad I was all my life." "Bad!" I responded. "What about all the good things you've done to help others. What about the prayers you said every day? You've always told God you were sorry for what you did wrong. Don't you think God has forgiven you?" "Oh, I guess so," she replied. "I'm just afraid of everything right now."

We talked and we wept together as she shared the many blessings and struggles of her life. Yes, she was eager to see her husband and God, too. Before I left we prayed about all the things she had shared. Her last words to me were: "How sweet of you to come. Thank you. I feel better now. I love you." With that she slipped into unconsciousness again and died the following day.

Wisdom Shared: "I doubt everything I ever believed."

Rhea and I had talked about our beliefs and values on many previous occasions. This gave her the confidence now, in her struggles, to share her doubts in her final moments of life. In life she always expressed her gratitude, and now in death she did not forget her "Thank you."

Now I Can Die in Peace

Patricia was at home and it was evident that the end was drawing near. Her two daughters and son had been with her for several weeks, and I had visited and prayed with her frequently. Early one morning I received a call saying Patricia wanted me to come as soon as I could. When I arrived at her home, she asked to be alone with me. She said: "I just cannot die until I know my children will be all right. Will you please do me a favor? Please talk to my oldest daughter and tell her not to be so concerned about money. It's ruining her life. Talk to my son and tell him to come back to the Church. How can he be happy without God? Ask my youngest daughter to let go of the grudge she is holding against her older sister. There is no peace." All I could do for a moment was to pray for help. Tears were rolling down Patricia's cheeks. I responded softly and slowly. "Patricia, do you think that you would have the strength to talk to each of your children privately and share with them the wish you have for them before you die?" We talked about how she might express these wishes. I prayed with her and left.

Another call came the following day asking me to come back. With arms entwined, the three children surrounded their mother's bed. Patricia had the wisdom, courage and strength to talk with each of her children. Her face showed a deep joy as she said: "Now I can die in peace." She died several days later.

Wisdom Shared: "I just cannot die until I know my children will be all right."

Patricia's love for her children was so strong that she wanted to do everything she could for them in their brokenness. She wanted them to find that their true purpose in life was to love God and one another. She was in instrument of God's peace.

Always Bringing Joy to Others

Throughout her life Margaret was always thinking about others and what might bring them happiness. She raised twelve beautiful children and knew how to anticipate their needs or desires. Now Margaret was in the hospital, close to death. Her children surrounded her bedside and I was with them. At one point Margaret called one of her daughters, Sister Rose Margaret, to her side, and with a twinkle in her eye, said to her: "Please give Sister Rita the wine from the cupboard at home, even the bottles that are opened. I know she likes wine."

Margaret lived life to the full and could find delight in giving even in the face of sadness.

Wisdom Shared: "I know she likes wine."

Margaret's life was lived bringing love and joy to everyone. The wine was a symbol of the joy she wanted to share. Is it any wonder that on her deathbed she thought of giving wine to someone whom she knew would enjoy it?

I Saw a Beautiful Angel

Carol was thirty-two years old and was dying of cancer. The greatest comfort she and her husband found was from reading Scripture and praying the psalms. John was struggling with the reality that Carol would soon die. Carol told John often: "I really don't want to die, but if God asks that of me now, I will say: 'Yes.'"

The day before Carol died she said to John: "Last night I saw a beautiful angel. I think the angel will take me soon." John's heart was comforted, and now he finally had the courage to say: "You can go now, Carol, and hang on to the angel's wings and fly into heaven." God sends angels to help us.

Wisdom Shared: "You can go now, Carol."

Carol and John searched for answers to their questions about Carol's sickness. With help from Scripture and through prayer they faced their situation with realism and arrived at full acceptance. God sends angels to be of help.

The Overwhelming Beauty of Heaven

Myra and Jack raised five children, one who died tragically in an industrial accident and four who now live in different states. On a Memorial Day weekend trip to his Iowa hometown to place flowers on his parent's graves, Jack had a heart attack and died while driving the car. This was a horrendous experience for Myra, who experienced the trauma of the car bounding across the highway and into the ditch. She suffered a broken sternum and other injuries. Soon after, Myra was diagnosed as having breast cancer. Another surgery weakened her body.

Myra is a heroic woman and through all this struggle her answer to people's questions about her health and well being was: "With God's help I'm doing very well, thank you. Now, tell me about yourself."

Then a blood disease that made her body retain iron caused Myra's liver to fail and she began filling up with fluid.

She said: "It is time for me to let go now, and I am not afraid to die. I am eager to see Jack and I am sure heaven is a wonderful place."

One day Myra told me that she had a dream and she saw Jack as an angel in heaven. As she said this she began to weep. Myra was never one to show her feelings publicly. I felt the deep stirring that was happening within her. When she became calm again, I asked: "What were you feeling when you saw Jack?" Myra replied: "I just wasn't ready for this." After a long pause she added: "The reality of heaven is so overwhelming and beautiful, that all I can do is weep when I think of it."

Wisdom Shared: "The reality of heaven is so overwhelming and beautiful."

We will not come to know here on earth what heaven is truly like, but there are ways we can come to realize that it must be truly beyond our imagining.

I'll Soon Be Pulling Daisies

Frances was eighty-one years old when she found out she had lung cancer. When she told me about this diagnosis she added: "You know, one has to look at the sunny side of life. I'm eighty-one years old and I could have had cancer at twenty-one years of age. I've had a very good life. I'm at peace. It is O.K."

Her positive attitude blossomed throughout her remaining days. One day I asked her if she would like to go outdoors to see the flowers. "No," she said, "that's O.K." Very soon I'll be pulling daises in heaven." She died several days later.

Wisdom Shared: "One has to look at the sunny side of life."

Frances had a simple and deep faith. She was childlike in her approach to God and always knew that God was on her side blessing her. She accepted what came her way and saw the goodness and beauty in life.

I'm Happy Inside

Art was a man of the circus and loved life. Now he was in a nursing home and couldn't do much any more. We used to have long talks about life and I asked him to teach me about what he thought were the important lessons of life. His favorite line was: "I'm not lonely because God is with me."

He taught me many things. He would say: "Life is great if you live right and always try to do what God wants you to do and take things as they come. If you have to suffer, remember that God doesn't send it but it is part of being human. I believe God weeps with me when I suffer."

He continues: "It looks like I am not doing anything as I lie here in bed, but even though my body is worn out and sick, I'm happy inside. I have great faith in God and I know God loves me and is with me. I really have a lot to do each day. I have a long list of people I'm praying for, and you are on my list. I think of you and pray for you every day."

Art always wanted to know what I was doing so he would know how to pray for me.

It was so important for him to do something for others. He also needed a friend and I felt so honored when he'd say: "It is wonderful to have a friend like you."

Wisdom Shared: "It looks like I'm not doing anything as I lie here in bed, but even though my body is worn out and sick, I'm happy inside."

All his life Art relied on God, on good days as well as on bad days. He depended on God's help in everything he did. He knew his life was precious even though he was incapacitated.

"Parties of the Heart"

Paul was a great Irishman and had such delightful ways of expressing himself. As he grew more feeble he had to give up his car, leave his home and move to an assisted living facility. He talked often about these changes. He would say: "Old age is a transition into a new way of being. I have to let go of doing things for myself, accept being slow, and the help of others. I look inside myself to see who I am. I look for the face of Jesus in those around me. I also have 'parties of the heart' every day. I read the Bible and often hear God telling me that I am important and loved." Paul knew the end was drawing near and exclaimed: "One of these days the trumpet will sound. I wait and I keep on living as best I can."

Wisdom Shared: "I read the Bible and often hear God telling me that I am important and loved."

Paul had learned one of the most important lessons in life, namely, that God's love for us is infinite. His whole life was lived out of this reality.

I Can Handle the Small Stuff

Kathy is a middle-aged woman dealing with cancer. Her words of wisdom have great truth: "I can handle the small stuff, but not the big stuff. But when I give the big stuff over to God, it becomes small stuff."

Wisdom Shared: "When I give the big stuff over to God, it becomes small stuff."

Kathy knows her need for God's help and power in her life. We need not walk alone, for God is with us on our journey.

Going Home Always Feels Good

Merle, who is active and involved, is not afraid to think about death. She says: "Going home always feel good. That's what I think it will be like to die and go to heaven."

"You know," she continues, "at home one has a safe place, it is familiar, relaxing and gives a sense of peace. One always loves to sleep in one's own bed, you know. We are comfortable being with people we know and love. Surely heaven will be a place like home and I'm sure there will also be plenty of joy and laughter."

Wisdom Shared: "One always loves to sleep in one's own bed."

If we are at home with God while here on earth, passing through death's door will surely feel like going home.

Give Some of Your Heart to Others

Father Wil has Parkinson's Disease, has had five back surgeries, knee surgeries and cancer. He is still very interested in everyone and everything and is involved in all aspects of life. Throughout his life he was very interested in people's lives and what was happening for them. With his compassionate heart he continues to reach out to anyone who is struggling in any way and also makes everyone feel important. It is wonderful to hear him say now: "People are so accepting of me in my illness. They make me feel needed and this is what keeps me going and gives me a reason to live. I am also happy to have the opportunity to continue celebrating the Liturgy. It makes me feel like I've 'gone to the mountain.' I feel stronger when I am there.

It is wonderful to have so many friends that haven't forgotten me. They visit me and remember me in many ways."

Father Wil says he's not afraid of death, but says: "I just wonder about many things: I wonder about where I will go right after I die; I wonder about what heaven is really like." It is good to wonder because mystery gives us strength.

Wisdom Shared: "It is wonderful to have so many friends that haven't forgotten me."

Whenever anyone comes into Father Wil's life he gives them some of his heart. He blesses everyone with his spirit and is like a magnet that draws one back over and over again to receive his blessing of love.

Jesus, Into Your Hands I Commend My Spirit

Father Jim's mother died when he was a little boy, and Jim and his twin brother spent time at a Children's Home since his father could not take care of the whole family. Jim became a priest, served as an army chaplain during World War II and the Korean War, became chaplain at a hospital, and served as a missionary for twenty-five years in Venezuela. With all his life experiences and the dangerous situations he encountered, he knew he had to depend on God's protection. One day he told me: "It must be wonderful when dying people tell you that they are looking forward to leaving this world and going into God's presence. I hope that when my time comes to die I will have that spirit. Every day I pray in anticipation of my dying, whether it will be this month or this year: 'Jesus, into your hands I commend my spirit.'"

Wisdom Shared: "Jesus, into your hands I commend my spirit."

We prepare so well for the activities that we anticipate in life. How wonderful to pray in anticipation of the day of our death.

The symbols and rituals of our Catholic faith make strong connections between the joys, sorrows, and hopes we experience in life. Recently five parishioners shared with the church community their insights into a particular symbol. The following are their stories.

Washing of Feet

Ed is thirty-nine years old and has Lou Gerhig's disease. He shares his reflections on the meaning of the symbol of washing feet that is part of the liturgical service on Holy Thursday. He begins with the Scriptural text:

"Jesus rose from the meal and took off his cloak. He picked up a towel and tied it around himself. Then he poured water into a basin and began to wash his disciples' feet and dry them with the towel he had around him. Thus he came to Simon Peter, who said to him: 'Lord, are you going to wash my feet?' Jesus answered, 'You may not realize now what I am doing, but later you will understand.' Peter replied: 'You shall never wash my feet!' 'If I do not wash you,' Jesus answered, 'you will have no share in my heritage.'" Jn. 13:3-8

Ed writes: " When I was healthy, just a couple of years ago, I was so much like Simon Peter. I was the one who wanted to help, to serve, to give, not only because Jesus taught me to serve, but also because it's far easier to give help than it is to need help. Why would I receive the service of others when I was healthy, strong, independent? To accept help was to admit a shortcoming, a vulnerability. It was fine to have others depend on me but not for me to depend on others. Peter and I know – it is easier to give than receive.

Well, things changed. At the age of thirty-five, I was diagnosed with Lou Gerhig's disease, a terminal condition with no treatment or cure. The symptoms, which began as minor nuisances and irritations, gradually changed me. The muscles in my body withered, first in my arms, then in my legs and neck. Simple tasks, like lifting a fork from a plate to my mouth became difficult, then impossible. One day I just gave in and quit trying, and now I find myself entirely dependent – hopelessly, tragically, and, in some ways, wonderfully dependent.

Like Peter, who reluctantly accepted Jesus' service after Jesus told him: 'Unless I wash you, you have no part with me,' I have learned to accept the help of others, and I believe I understand what Jesus was saying to Peter.

By allowing others to wash my feet I accept my weakness and it is a humbling experience. From my vantage of profound humility, I see now how difficult it can be to know Jesus until I accept the power of his comfort as found in the kindness and voluntary service of the members of the community of God. We are made in the image of God, and in service to one another we follow the example of Jesus. This I knew, but in my bravado and perceived independence I didn't see then what I see so clearly now, that it is my feet being washed. In my weakness I have found humility and in humility I see Jesus' presence in those who help me.

The symbol of Jesus washing the feet of his disciples is so gentle, caring, and beautifully simple. In good health it was a call to serve others. In illness it is a reminder of my dependency on others. He promised to be with us when we are scared and without hope. To me he shows his commitment to that promise through the kindness of those who help me. As members of God's community we teach our children that it's better to give than to receive, but I believe it is best to give and receive because in giving, washing the feet of others, we act like Christ, and in receiving, allowing others to wash our feet, we see him."

The Cross

Kevin, a high school teacher, shares what the symbol of the cross means to him. Since his childhood he participated in the Holy Week Liturgies and especially remembers the Good Friday Services and the veneration of the cross. The faith community that revealed the meaning of the cross to him most fully was made up of emotionally disturbed youth, ages eight to eighteen, with whom he worked as a youth minister.

Kevin writes: "I remember the first weeks of meeting, visiting and playing with the thirty students. They seemed a lot like any other young persons I had ever met, that is, until I read some of their files. I read about Jeff, whose father would discipline him by taking a lit cigarette and putting it out — I mean, grinding it out — on Jeff's arm. I read about Sarah, who from the age of two and a half, would often hide in her closet, hoping desperately that her dad would not find her again and have sex with her. I read about Jose, whose mother often punished him by kicking him down the stairs. I began to wonder, to deeply wonder — how can there be a God if such incredible suffering by innocent people exists? And some of the lines I remember hearing as I was growing up — about how God never gives us more than we can handle, or that we all have our crosses to bear — just didn't work any more.

For those of you who have experienced such heartfelt questions and doubts about whether or not God exists — and where God is — you know how troubling it can be, how challenging it is to be uncertain about something you had previously assumed was true; and it's even more complicated when you have a job that requires that you try to help other people to believe that the God whom you now doubt is real.

There were people who told me I was losing my faith — but I found that when I tried to deny what I was going through, the questions and uncertainty pursued me. So I became very honest about the struggle — decided not to say the creed during Mass and chose, at times, not to come forward to communion. I read and prayed the Scriptures. There were passages that began to resonate within me in a new and deeper way. Jesus' agony in the Garden — the plea for his friends to stay awake, the drops of blood he sweat and his cry to God to let this cup pass him by — seemed to express the kinds of agony I heard in the students' stories. The torture of the whips and of the nails through his hands and feet, and His cry from the cross – "My God, my God, why have You abandoned me?" – now seemed to be re-echoed in the brutality in so many students' lives.

I think I realized for the first time in my life how evil the cross really is – that neither the cigarette burns on Jeff's arms nor the wounds in Jesus' hands and feet are good, that Sarah's agony in the closet and Jesus' agony in the garden are deeply destructive, and that God did not cause or even desire Jesus' broken heart and spirit any more than God caused or desired the brokenness of Jose tumbling down the stairs.

The cross is deeply, totally evil – and God embraced it, and by so doing, God revealed how deeply God has entered into human life, and how the loving, life-giving energy of God can enable us to travel through the cross, into resurrected life.

That is what I have come to see now when I look at the cross – a reality that is so completely evil that God has fully experienced, and promises to accompany us through.

I see the cross everywhere. I see it in the stories of students and adults who take the risk to reach out to be with people who are marginalized – to get to know people who are homeless, to listen to the experiences of someone discriminated against for their race or sexual orientation, to learn from a person in a nursing home or someone struggling through a GED class. I see it in the lives, death and witness of young people like Julianne Williams, a young woman from our parish whose life was so unjustly ended at a campsite in Shenandoah National Park, or Sam Keaveny, the young man who died suddenly in the emergency room last spring. I see it in my family's experience of my clinical depression two years ago – a year-long journey about which I have very few memories, but about which my wife has vivid ones – memories that can be triggered unexpectedly by a song on the radio, a glance at a calendar – memories that can reappear at any time, day or night, and cause her to spend time weeping.

The cross reminds me that Julie's murder and Sam's death are evil – that my depression and the incredible trauma it brought to my family and friends was deeply wrong – that the marginalization of people is neither God-caused nor God-desired. The cross reminds me that God embraced a way of life that contained such pain – and rose from it – and invited us to travel the same path – and that doing so mysteriously, ultimately makes sense, mysteriously and ultimately leads to a fullness of life that can never be destroyed."

Eucharistic Bread

Marilyn, a deeply faith-filled woman of the parish, has served as a baker of Eucharistic Bread for eighteen years. The week before Holy Week she told parishioners what it means to her to prepare the Eucharistic Bread for Liturgy.

"From the first time I baked the Eucharistic Bread and every time after, I have felt a kind of awe. I considered my ministry a true and definite honor because it allows me to be instrumental in preparing the bread that will become the Body of Christ at the Eucharist. I have never baked the bread without beginning by saying a prayer for assistance from above. And when I am finished, I pray a prayer of thanks. I pray that everyone who receives the bread of Eucharist will feel the presence and power of Jesus.

Water: Beautiful and Dangerous

Chris, liturgist and musician for over twenty-five years, shares his reflections on the symbol of water.

"Living in Minnesota we are constantly touched by water, six feet of snow, ten thousand lakes and one of the world's greatest rivers, the Mississippi, which runs through our city. I came to Minnesota, drawn by lakes, and that's where I learned that water is beautiful and dangerous.

I have often sat on the banks of the Mississippi, watching the sunset, being dazzled by the light dancing on the waters. I enjoyed kayaking the gentle waves in midsummer, kicking off my shoes and putting my feet in the cool waters. These were times of refreshment — so life-giving, so beautiful.

I also remember the day when the floods came and houses were being engulfed and ripped from their foundations. The waters turned dark, ugly, with massive chunks of ice swirling, tree trunks rolling, crashing through the whirlpools and waves. I stood far away watching, yet was drawn to get closer and closer to touch those waters. They were alluring and deadly. They enticed me and scared me. They were so dangerous. Yes, water is so life-giving, beautiful and also so dangerous.

As we enter our church we instantly hear the sound of water. Adults, children and infants enter our faith through the waters of this font. These are waters that are beautiful, that bring life, and are also so dangerous.

When my wife, Patty, and I immersed our daughter and son in those baptismal waters, we committed ourselves to raising them as God's children. We committed ourselves to teaching them who God is, who Jesus is, who the Spirit is. We committed ourselves to be an example of what a Christian is, what a Catholic is and what it means to love. This commitment is dangerous, because it so often means that we have to let go of ourselves, our desires, our control.

Every time we touch those waters, we recommit ourselves to living our own Baptismal promises: to live a life that is holy, that is good, to turn away from evil in whatever form it takes today, to live a life of service, a life that trusts God, and that is beautiful and that is dangerous. Water is life-giving, refreshing, beautiful and so dangerous."

Oil of Anointing

Donna faithfully stood by her husband's, side during ten years of illness. She suffered with Frank as she witnessed his pain. She wrote the following reflection about what the Sacrament of the Sick means to her.

"I want you to picture an intensive care unit where a family awaits the return of a much loved husband and father from surgery. Suddenly he's there. We try to hide the horror we feel as we look to the spot where his leg used to be, and we try to mask the terrible ache we feel witnessing his pain. Then amidst the hustle and bustle of transferring him from gurney to bed, a chaplain appears. In my benumbed state it takes a second to register why he is there. 'Would Frank like the Sacrament of Healing?' he asks us. Frank answers for himself.

"As the calming words of the sacrament flow over him, we can see him relax. Through my head runs the Baltimore Catechism definition of a sacrament – 'an outward sign, instituted by Christ, to give grace.' Somehow, I felt safer as I listened. Sad as I was, I was happy, too, to belong to a Church which reached out to us. I felt more at peace, but, of course, all this would be meaningless without faith, and I thanked God for giving us that gift.

"Just as the medicine given to him to try to heal his body, this symbol acts as medicine for his soul – a healing of the spirit. Some of the 'why' questions I had—Why must a good man endure so much suffering? Why would God allow it?—began to be replaced with a deeper understanding. Our earthly bodies wear out in different ways. This sacrament to me is one of hope – hope for an everlasting life, free of pain.

"How wise the Church is to give us these signs and symbols to see us through the ups and downs of life. No, there was no miraculous, physical cure for Frank. In its place we received the grace to accept whatever God had in store for us."

God has gifted us through the world of nature, in the world of humanity and the world of the spirit. If we take the time, we will be able to appreciate the marvels that are ours to enjoy and come to understand the meaning of suffering.

It is then we can share with one another the greatest gifts in life that come from the deep inner treasury of the human heart.

A note to the reader...

Sister Rita Barthel lived with vitality, energy and good humor. She frequently "wasted time with people," and was often the last person to leave a meeting or a party. When dropping something off at a home, she didn't hesitate to stay for a cup of tea. She had an amazing ability to connect with people at a deep level, as was evidenced at her wake and funeral where so many testified that they experienced her as "a very special friend."

Rita found it difficult to work with those who were dying, speaking about the agony, not only of the dying person, but also of those who accompanied this person on their journey. As she saw people die with courage and abandonment, she anguished over whether she had the courage to enter into the pain and suffering and see it through to the finish. Rita shared her doubts, fears and struggles, telling others that she wanted to run the race and go the distance. "What I wished [for her]" said a friend, "was a real peacefulness. What surprised me was how quickly she died. She was like a feather being thrown into the sky and swept away by the wind"

Throughout her dying process, which went very quickly, parish members, friends, family and her Sisters supported S. Rita. Even as she grew weaker, ministry continued to be important to her and she consciously sought ways to serve others. She reached out to the hospital staff during those last weeks, learning their names and something personal about each of them. She thanked them for caring for her and offered them small gifts. "How humble she was in receiving physical care," said one friend. "There seemed to be a transformation [in her] as she moved toward another form of life."

Rita's parish friends wrote a "book" of messages for her, many of which referred to encounters Rita had with them while ministering to one of their family members. Each day someone read aloud to her one of the thoughts from that book, then placed it back in its designated spot so it could easily be found the next day.

Once diagnosed, Rita sensed that she did not have long to live. Shortly before she died, she expressed her longing for death and that she had no regrets. She welcomed Sister Death in the spirit of a true Franciscan, knowing that a life of love opened her to the greater life promised by God. In her death as in her life, she was a faithful servant of our loving God.

Sister Bea Eichten

Sister Beatrice Eichten, OSF
Community Minister

About the author

Sister Rita Barthel, OSF
March 29, 1931 – July 18, 2003

Sister Rita Barthel lived her life as a Franciscan Sister of Little Falls, Minnesota. Throughout her life, Sister Rita embraced a wide variety of experiences — as a teacher, a school principal, a missionary in the slums of Venezuela, and as a pastoral associate in several Catholic parishes. She was also active in a number of leadership positions within her Franciscan community. Sister Rita earned a bachelor's degree from the College of St. Catherine in St. Paul, Minnesota; a Masters Degree in Spirituality from the University of San Francisco; and a Masters Degree in Theology from the University of Toronto.

At the time of her death, Sister Rita was working as a pastoral associate at the Church of St. Paul in St. Cloud, Minnesota. She directed the parish Befriender Program, coordinated retreats and outreach ministries, and served as a spiritual guide to those seeking guidance. She ministered without counting the cost to herself and had a deep love for the sick and dying. Sister Rita wrote FINDING LIFE'S PURPOSE, WHERE DO I ENCOUNTER GOD? during the last years of her life. Her thoughts and insights flowed from her Franciscan spirituality. This book was a way for her to share that spirituality with others. Sister Rita also hoped that the book would pass along the wisdom and faith of her family, friends, and of the many people she ministered with during the years.

Sister Rita's faith, her love of life, her laughter and care, made a difference in many lives. She will be missed, but those who knew her will find ways to carry on her good work.

"Those I leave behind will carry on
and will know that love never dies."

~ Sister Rita Barthel, OSF ~

An Invitation to Journal...

    As Sister Rita wrote in her introduction, FINDING LIFE'S PURPOSE, WHERE DO I ENCOUNTER GOD? is a book to be pondered.

    These additional pages are provided for your personal journaling and reflection about your own journey of faith...

An Invitation to Journal...

An Invitation to Journal...

An Invitation to Journal...

An Invitation to Journal...

An Invitation to Journal...

An Invitation to Journal...

An Invitation to Journal...